BOY, WERE WE WRONG
— ABOUT THE —
SOLAR SYSTEM!

Kathleen V. Kudlinski ILLUSTRATED BY John Rocco

DUTTON CHILDREN'S BOOKS

To planetariums, where I first fell in love
with star science
K.V.K.

For my parents
J.R.

DUTTON CHILDREN'S BOOKS • A division of Penguin Young Readers Group

Published by the Penguin Group
Penguin Group (USA) Inc., 375 Hudson Street, New York, New York 10014, U.S.A. • Penguin Group (Canada),
90 Eglinton Avenue East, Suite 700, Toronto, Ontario, M4P 2Y3 Canada (a division of Pearson Penguin Canada
Inc.) • Penguin Books Ltd, 80 Strand, London WC2R 0RL, England • Penguin Group Ireland, 25 St Stephen's
Green, Dublin 2, Ireland (a division of Penguin Books Ltd) • Penguin Group (Australia), 250 Camberwell Road,
Camberwell, Victoria 3124, Australia (a division of Pearson Australia Group Pty Ltd) • Penguin Books India
Pvt Ltd, 11 Community Centre, Panchsheel Park, New Delhi—110 017, India • Penguin Group (NZ), 67 Apollo
Drive, Rosedale, North Shore 0632, New Zealand (a division of Pearson New Zealand Ltd) • Penguin Books
(South Africa) (Pty) Ltd, 24 Sturdee Avenue, Rosebank, Johannesburg 2196, South Africa • Penguin Books Ltd,
Registered Offices: 80 Strand, London WC2R 0RL, England

CIP Data is available.

Published in the United States by Dutton Children's Books, a division of Penguin Young Readers Group
345 Hudson Street, New York, New York 10014 • www.penguin.com/youngreaders

Designed by Jason Henry

Manufactured in China • First Edition • ISBN: 978-0-525-46979-7
10 9 8 7 6 5 4 3 2 1

Long, long ago, before people knew anything about the solar system, they saw the sun move in the sky. The moon moved, too. People watched the stars make a grand slow circle in the sky every night. But their world didn't seem to move at all.

They thought everything in the heavens moved around their flat, steady Earth. Boy, were they wrong!

We now know that we live on a little planet that moves with other worlds around a medium-size sun in a large galaxy. But it took a long time and a lot of wrong guesses to learn what we now know today.

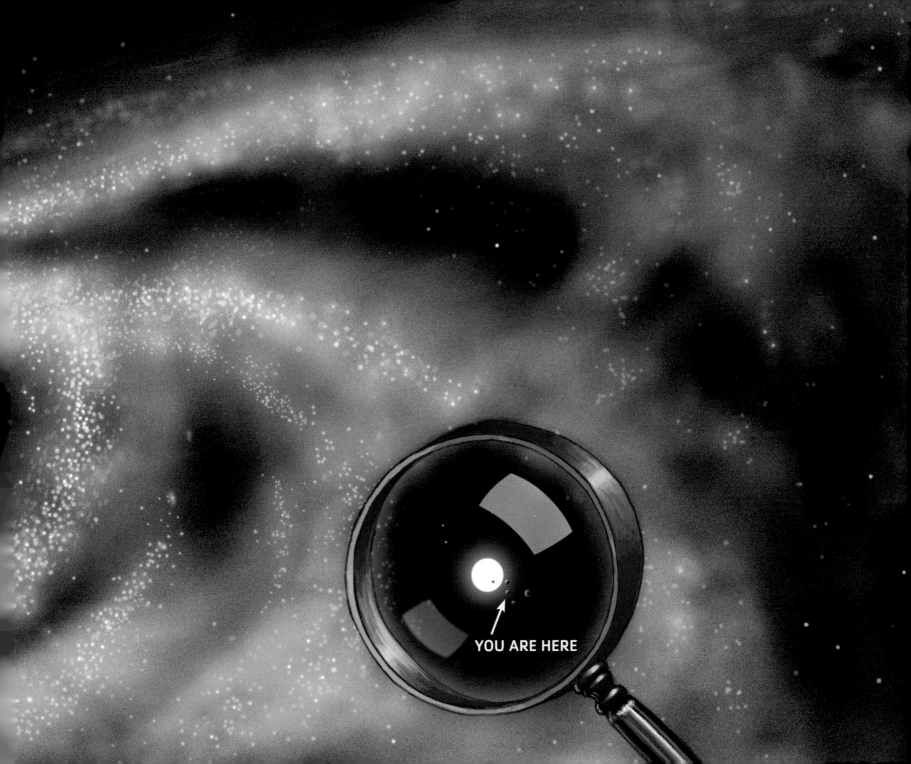

YOU ARE HERE

Early people saw that a few stars did not twinkle. These glowing dots moved differently than all the others circling the night sky. People named these special wanderers after their gods—Jupiter, Venus, Saturn, Mercury, and Mars.

The moon also moved and it changed shape in the sky. When the Earth came between the sun and the moon, it cast a round shadow on the moon. The early Greeks realized that since the Earth's shadow was round, then the Earth must be round, too.

People invented new tools to study the skies and measure where and when the planets moved. They made sky maps, too, and at last they saw a system to the heavens.

The stars, they said, were dots on a huge clear ball. Inside that glassy ball the planets and the sun occupied smaller and smaller spheres. Earth was the all-important center of everything.

They thought that the heavens were perfect and everlasting.

Boy, were they wrong about our solar system!

One man watched a comet slide right through where the Moon's sphere was supposed to be—and nothing happened. No glass ball shattered. The clear spheres weren't really there. The planets must just be floating through space.

Another astronomer saw a brand-new star appear one night. It didn't go away. Many others saw it, too. If new stars could appear, then maybe the heavens weren't unchanging.

A new idea came to an astronomer. He said the sun was in the center of the system, not the Earth. That would mean that we were not so important. He had no proof, so most people just laughed at the idea of a sun-centered system. Boy, were they wrong!

The first telescopes changed everything. Looking through them, astronomers could see that things in the heavens were not perfect, after all. The sun had spots. The moon had mountains and craters, and Saturn appeared to be lumpy.

And everyone could see for the first time that Venus changed shape just like our moon. That meant sunlight was shining on it from many different angles. Venus had to be circling the sun! If that was true, the other planets must be circling the sun, too. The Earth was not the center of the universe!

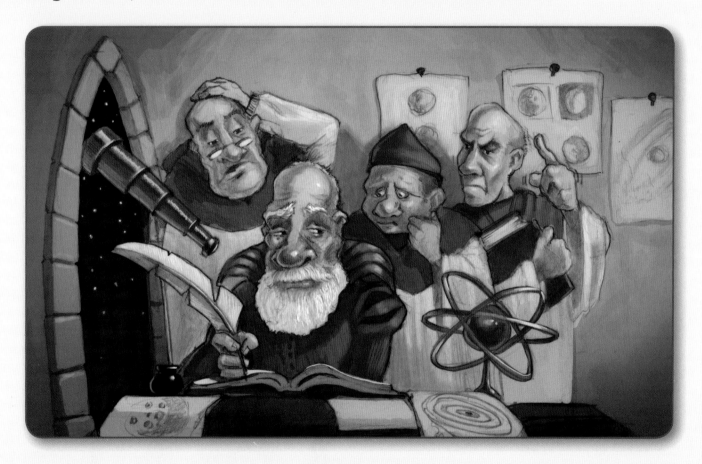

Church leaders thought these new findings went against the Bible. They had a famous scientist arrested when he wrote about the discoveries. He could never come to church again. But nothing they said could change the facts.

Another scientist watched an apple fall. It made him think. Why didn't apples fall sideways or up? He decided Earth had a gravity force that pulled apples and everything else toward it. Maybe Earth's gravity was pulling as far as the moon. And maybe the moon pulled us right back. Planets could tug on each other, too.

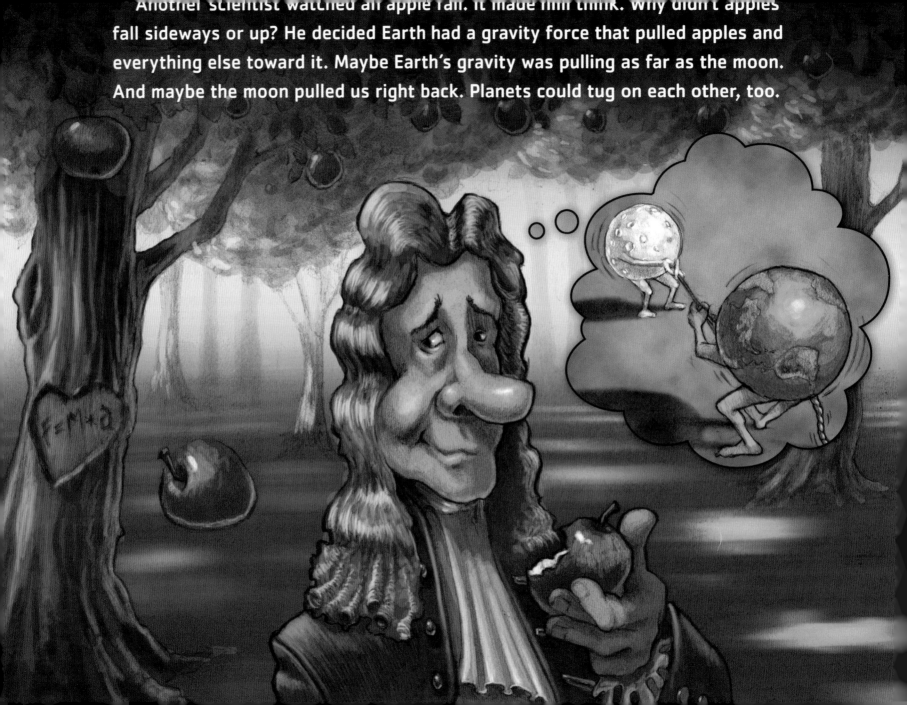

Scientists checked the measurements and it seemed to be true. Gravity made the planets shift when they passed each other. But Saturn shifted for no reason. Astronomers wondered if there was another planet out there. When they pointed their telescopes toward the source of gravity, they found Neptune.

Better telescopes showed that the lumps on Saturn were really rings—and a few moons, too. Scientists thought that maybe Saturn's gravity was pulling a ring-shaped cloud of tiny rocks to itself. They were swinging around too fast to fall down—gravity had them trapped in an orbit.

A long time ago...

Thirty-seven years later...

Thirty-seven years later...

Astronomers looked at the old charts of comets and saw one that kept coming back about every thirty-seven years. They looked at its path. They figured in the gravity of the planets it passed and told the world exactly when to expect the comet to show up next. People laughed—but the comet showed up right on time. Everything seemed to be making sense now.

As the telescopes got even better, anyone could see that Mars had two moons. And in the big space between Mars and Jupiter there was a whole cloud of loose rocks orbiting the sun. What else would they find? They saw great seas on Mars, too, and channels where water flowed. Some people thought it must have taken thousands of smart Martians to dig these huge canals. Boy, were they wrong!

More detailed pictures of the Martian surface showed channels that had been carved out by ancient rushing rivers. Those rivers and seas seemed to be dry now. People could see that Neptune's path wobbled, too. Could there be yet another planet in our solar system? When astronomers looked, they found Uranus.

Photography changed everything again. An astronomer found tiny little Pluto on a photograph long before anyone saw it in the sky. "I have found a new planet!" he announced. Schoolchildren learned that there were nine planets in all. Maps and models showed Pluto the planet. It was official for more than seventy years.

Then more tiny planets were found, and more. There seemed to be a whole belt of them circling the sun wildly beyond Neptune. Were they *all* planets?

Astronomers took a vote. "No," they said, "Pluto is just a dwarf planet. So are all the others like it."

Boy, were *we* wrong about Pluto.

Another new tool detected chemicals from a distance. Astronomers did not have to visit Jupiter or Venus to learn that their atmospheres had poison gases instead of Earth-like air.

They also built a system of giant telescopes that used radio waves instead of light waves to look into space. They put them far away from city noises so they would not interfere with the sounds of space.

These radio telescopes peered right through the clouds of other planets and we could learn even more details. There were huge mountains under those poison clouds on Venus. Under Jupiter's clouds, there was nothing but more clouds.

Other scientists sent a satellite into space. When that worked, they sent dogs up, then a monkey. Then they sent a man.

The first astronaut finally saw the stars without having to look through Earth's thick layer of air.

TAKE OFF!

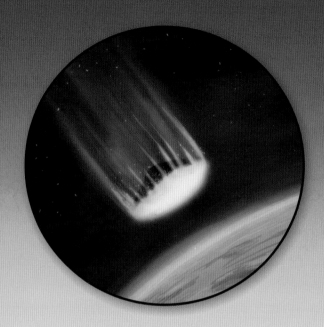

HURTLING TOWARD MARS

Other astronomers designed instruments to fly through the solar system. Some probes flew close enough to see that the head of a comet was just a dirty ice ball. Others landed on the surface of Mars.

A BUMPY LANDING

READY TO ROLL!

THAT WAS A LONG RIDE. I HOPE THERE IS SOME WATER AROUND HERE.

Scientists made a digital telescope with a huge lens eight feet across. They sent this telescope into orbit to take photographs of our solar system. At first it did not work. Astronauts had to fly up to repair it.

After being fixed, the telescope has sent back pictures of comets crashing into Jupiter's poison clouds and recorded a ring of a hundred million comets circling our solar system. It has even showed us proof of a whole solar system circling another star.

Our ideas will change as we learn more. Scientists keep inventing better instruments. Every year more advanced probes are sent through the solar system. There are plans to rocket people out among the planets and even to land on them.

No one has ever seen our whole solar system—or even a photograph of it. One day, someone will be sent out to look back at it from the outside. And someday, someone will visit other solar systems we've seen.

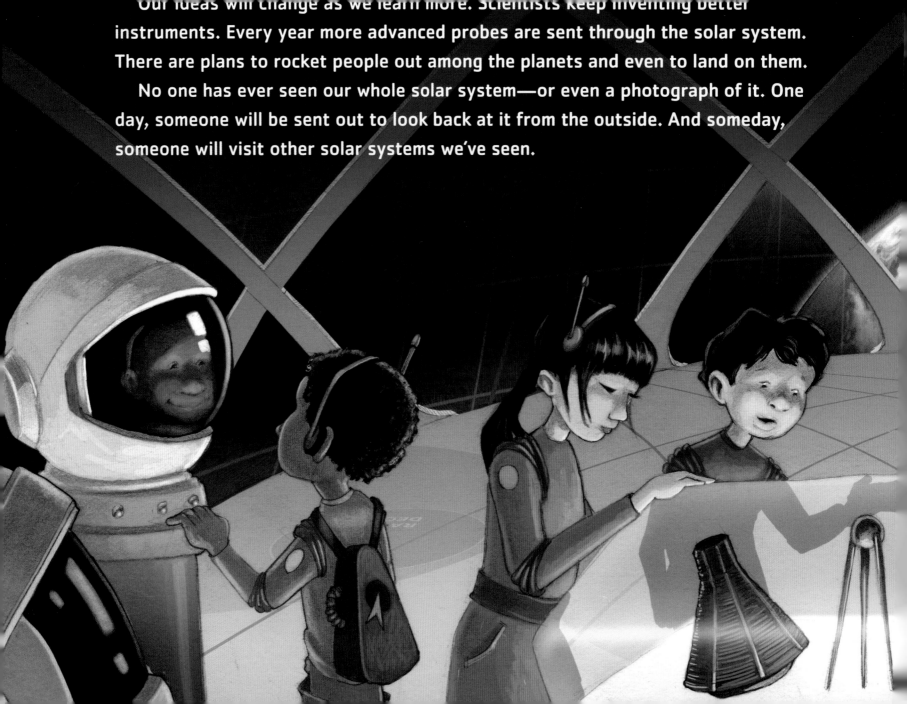

What will we learn? It will probably surprise us. Perhaps you will be one of the scientists—or one of the astronauts—who makes us say, "Boy, were we wrong about the solar system!"

A SOLAR SYSTEM DISCOVERY TIME LINE

600 BC Pythagoras recognizes that the Earth is round

400 BC Eudoxus makes the models of the spheres

400 BC Aristotle—everything in the heavens is perfect; planets, paths, unchanging

1543 Copernicus says the sun is central to the solar system

1577 Tycho Brahe finds comet to be part of heavens, not just weather

1609 Kepler figures out the squashed circle shape of planets' paths through space

1632 Galileo, using telescopes, makes arguments proving the sun is central

1655 Christian Huygens says Saturn has moons—and rings

1687 Newton finds spectrum of white light and works out theory of gravity, predicts return of Halley's comet (in 1759 comet returns on schedule)

1781 William Herschel discovers Uranus

1846 Neptune is discovered

1864 Giovanni Donati looks at light from comet with spectroscope

1957 First satellite launched from Earth (Soviet Union, now known as Russia)

1969 First man on the moon

1990 Hubble Telescope launched but doesn't work right (fixed in 1993)

2006 Pluto is demoted to a dwarf planet by the Astronomical Union
       More dwarf planets are discovered in the Kuiper Belt past Neptune

---

WHERE YOU CAN LOOK FOR MORE INFORMATION

Fradin, Dennis Brindell. *The Planet Hunters: The Search for Other Worlds*. Simon & Schuster, NY, NY, 1997.   Richly illustrated for kids with more questions.

Parker, Steve. *Galileo and the Universe*. Harper Collins, NY, NY, 1995.

Ibid. *Isaac Newton and Gravity*. Chelsea House, NY, NY, 1995.

These books are in-depth and lively, giving more depth to the scientists and their times.

http://kids.msfc.nasa.gov/   The NASA site for kids, full of amazing info, games, graphics, and the most recent news from the Hubble telescope.

http://ology.amnh.org/astronomy   The American Museum of Natural History site for kids about astronomy. Easy to navigate and fun!

A FEW OF THE SOURCES USED IN THE RESEARCH FOR THIS BOOK

Hoskin, Michael, ed. *The Cambridge History of Astronomy*. Cambridge University Press, NY, NY, 1997.   Richly illustrated thorough text for adults.

Motz, Lloyd, and Jefferson Hane Weaver. *The Story of Astronomy*. Perseus Publishing, Cambridge, MA, 1995.   A good overview for adult readers.

http//:stsci.edu   NASA's Hubble site